LIFE IN
A WARTIME
HOUSE
1939–1945

BRIAN WILLIAMS

The morning after an air raid: residents of
this London street survey the damage and
count the cost in September 1940.

1938 The Women's Voluntary Service (WVS) is formed. Air Raid Precautions (ARP) are announced.

August 1939 Blackout trial in London. The Emergency Powers (Defence) Act gives the government additional powers in the event of war.

1 September 1939 German troops invade Poland.

3 September 1939 Britain and France at war with Germany. Evacuation from cities underway.

29 September 1939 The National Register means every person is issued with an identity card.

January 1940 Food rationing: butter, bacon and sugar are first to be rationed, followed in March by meat.

May 1940 German armies invade Belgium, Netherlands and France. Neville Chamberlain resigns as Britain's Prime Minister and Winston Churchill forms a coalition government.

May 1940 The Local Defence Volunteers, later renamed the Home Guard, set up amid fears of invasion.

May–June 1940 British troops are evacuated from Dunkirk. France falls.

June–September 1940 The Battle of Britain.

7 September 1940 The Blitz on London begins; nearly 1.5 million Londoners are made homeless between September 1940 and May 1941.

14/15 November 1940 The Blitz on Coventry; during the winter of 1940–41 many other cities across the United Kingdom are bombed.

March 1941 Registration of Employment laws direct women into war work or the services.

June 1941 Clothes rationing starts. Two million British homes are listed as destroyed or damaged. German armies invade the Soviet Union.

September 1941 Utility clothing control order legislation passed by the government and the Utility quality mark CC41 is first seen.

7 December 1941 The Japanese attack Pearl Harbor and the United States joins the war.

February 1942 Soap is rationed to one tablet per month. No petrol for private use.

July 1942 Sweets are rationed.

October 1942 Milk ration is cut to 2½ pints (1.2 litres) a week per person. Bathwater is restricted to 5 inches (12.5cm).

January 1943 Utility furniture catalogue published. Conscription age for single women lowered to 19.

April 1943 Women join the Home Guard for the first time. Campaigns for salvage (recycling) and 'make do and mend' are stepped up during 1943.

March 1944 Plans for 500,000 prefabricated 'temporary' homes are announced.

6 June 1944 D-Day: Allied forces land in Normandy. During June–August 1944, London and southern England are hit by German V1 and V2 missiles.

September 1944 The blackout is lifted after five years.

7 May 1945 Germany surrenders; end of the war in Europe.

26 July 1945 Labour wins the general election and forms a new government.

September 1945 Japan surrenders; the Second World War ends.

THE WARTIME HOUSE

In the Second World War (1939–45) the people of Britain found their homes in the front line. Cities became targets for bombs, and just as houses and flats were wrecked by fire and high explosive, so too were families broken, hopes dashed, loves lost. For people under daily and nightly stress, home became a refuge and a rallying point; their homes were what they were fighting to protect. The war swept away some old barriers: united in a common cause, people mingled more freely, spoke to neighbours, helped passers-by and welcomed strangers into their homes – as refugees, evacuees, bomb-victims, or passing acquaintances in need of a sit-down and a cup of tea. At home everyone got used to 'going without' and the domestic battlefield was littered with the munitions of a new kind of war: air-raid shelters, blackout curtains, ration books, stirrup pumps, gas masks, cold dinners, chilly baths, hand-knitted socks, pig bins, Utility furniture and Woolton pie.

When in 1945 houses across Britain were hung with flags to celebrate victory, people could see only too clearly the damage that six years of war had wrought, with gaping holes where streets and homes once stood. In the heady days of celebration, people dreamed of new towns and streets, new homes in a brave new world. The most optimistic dreams were unrealized, but the landscape of Britain today reflects decisions taken by post-war planners, faced with the challenge of rebuilding a nation for which the wartime house had become a symbol of its people's endurance under fire.

The cheerful side of clearing up. Women in Bromley, Kent, smile for the camera as they salvage belongings from bombed-out houses.

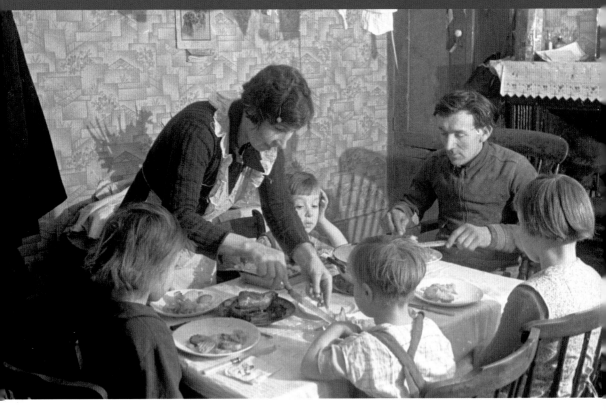

In March 1938 Home Secretary Sir Samuel Hoare broadcast to Britain. 'If the emergency arose, I know you would come in your hundreds of thousands,' he intoned, calling for volunteers to become air-raid wardens. His appeal at first attracted little response. It was only 20 years since the end of the Great War, 'the war to end wars', when the victors had spoken of a new world harmony and 'homes for heroes'. Yet the 1920s and 1930s had brought only an uneasy peace, the Great Depression and the rise of Hitler in Nazi Germany. People were not ready for another war.

By 1938, with the worst of the world economic recession over, factories were busy again and housebuilding was booming. More than 4 million new homes had been built since the First World War; in 1938 a couple setting up home could buy a suburban semi-detached house for under £600, taking a mortgage with a building society. Councils were building homes for rent. The London County Council had 86,000 such homes and nearly 400,000

tenants, on estates such as Becontree in Essex (120,000 people in 1939), and Downham in south-east London, which for its 29,000 residents had just one cinema and one pub.

Rows of new private homes sprawled onto green fields and along stretches of coast. The semi-detached homes and bungalows irritated 'progressive' architects; commercial builders and most buyers shunned 'modernist' homes (functional, undecorated and open-plan) in favour of mock-Tudor (or mock something else) with brick walls, pitched tiled roofs, bay windows with wooden frames, glass-panelled front doors, small gardens and garages. To their owners, these homes offered a mix of uniformity and individuality. The 'semi' was compact: unlike many a Victorian town house it had no rooms for servants – only the rich could still afford maids and cooks. Smaller still were older terraced houses and workers' cottages, home to millions in town and country; some pre-1914 homes lacked inside toilets and bathrooms,

◄ In 1939 Britain was still getting back to work after the Depression. This family had a wage packet again: after three years on the dole, dad got a job digging air-raid trenches following a *Picture Post* magazine article highlighting his plight.

► 1930s Britain hoped for years of peace. A home of one's own was the dream of millions – a dream that was encouraged by housebuilders and advertisers.

▲ Government advertising took on a sombre tone. This poster gave reminders for a going-to-bed routine during air raids.

and had gaslight rather than electricity, but the worst of the 19th-century slums had been replaced by council houses and flats.

In September 1938 Prime Minister Neville Chamberlain flew back from his Munich meeting with Adolf Hitler, clutching a 'peace' agreement. Few believed he had won anything other than a breathing-space. The question was not if war would come, but when. Londoners gazed up at barrage balloons and wondered about the safety of their homes. In demonstrations of civic readiness, borough emergency services displayed their skills, banners proclaiming that 'national service is the business of the citizen'.

The wail of air-raid sirens on 3 September 1939 confirmed worst fears: it was war. Commuters glanced at press advertisements with fresh interest: concrete shelters available from £30; £5 extra if semi-sunk. The peacetime house was about to become the wartime house.

PROVIDENCE MADE REAL

Typical of 1930s municipal flats was Providence House in Poplar, east London. Built in 1935, as part of a slum-clearance scheme, this five-storey block had 80 flats, each with a bathroom and hot water from a boiler, and there was a communal washing-line in the courtyard. A two-bedroom flat cost 11s 6d (57p) a week; a three-bedroom flat 13s 6d (67p). Providence House survived the war, with some damage, but was demolished in 1981.

► A wartime National Registration identity card. On 29 September 1939, National Registration Day, every household had to fill in forms giving details of all occupants. Everyone had to carry an identity card: green for adults, brown for under-16s.

At first people were bombarded by the Ministry of Information: told how to dig trenches; how to place sandbags to shield windows; how to douse fires with a stirrup pump; how to dispose of incendiary bombs with a scoop and sand-bucket. Shelter-trenches in public spaces were for use only by 'people passing through the streets'. Those who could, should go home – provided they could do so within five minutes. Others should shelter at their workplace.

For months nothing much happened. This was the 'Phoney War': no bombs fell, cinemas reopened and life went on more or less as usual. In the spring and summer of 1940, war became real: the Nazis overran Norway, Denmark and the Low Countries; after Dunkirk came the fall of France, the threat of invasion, the Battle of Britain and the start of the Blitz. Air raids on Britain's cities began in earnest in September 1940. In London at the peak of the Blitz about 150,000 people sheltered nightly in Underground stations. Night after night cities across the country became targets.

The most widely used home shelter was the Anderson, named after Sir John Anderson, the architect of air-raid protection before the war. Two million Anderson shelters were issued; they cost £7, but were free to people earning less than £5 a week. Measuring 6½ by 4½ feet (2 x 1.4m), the corrugated-steel arched shelter was partly buried in a hole up to 4 feet (1.2m) deep, then covered with soil. It was remarkably bomb-proof (unless suffering a direct hit) but tended to flood after rain, which made sheltering a chilly experience – even with flasks of tea, blankets and hot-water bottles.

Fearing enemy planes would drop poison gas as well as high explosive, the government advised people to turn one room into a gas-proof 'refuge room', and issued 38 million gas masks. Women's League of Health and Beauty members cavorted in

➤ This Anderson shelter was an obstacle as its owner pegged out the washing in her backyard in January 1940.

AIR RAID PRECAUTIONS
WHAT TO DO IN
EMERGENCY
6ᵈ

A COMPREHENSIVE GUIDE IN GRAPHIC NARRATIVE

The Jones Family Sees it Through
By JOHN LANGDON-DAVIES

The Refuge Room
How to Make Garden Trenches
The Construction of Surface Shelters
The Warden Service
Rescue Parties and the Clearance of Debris
The Auxiliary Fire Service
First Aid Posts and Ambulance Services
The Decontamination Squad

▲ Commercial publishers and the Ministry of Information issued guides on what to do when enemy bombers began to blast the suburbs. Hardly comforting bedtime reading, though much of the advice was reasonably practical.

➤ This W.D. & H.O. Wills cigarette picture card showed families how to equip a 'refuge room': with water, sand-box, stirrup pump, bedding and (discreetly peeking from a half-open door) a chamber pot.

gas masks, to encourage their use, but most people hated wearing them. The masks had to be kept cool and dry, so shops tried to sell containers 'to protect your gas mask against bad weather'. As the fear of gas attack receded, many masks were left at home to become post-war mementoes.

The Morrison shelter for indoor use appeared in 1941. It was basically a steel cage, holding four people at a squeeze. Its flat top was good for table tennis and it made a fine den for children's games, but it was a lifesaver too. Under the stairs was the next safest place at home; in a cellar, people feared being buried under rubble. As the Blitz went on, more people defiantly or recklessly stayed indoors, trying to ignore the racket outside.

▲ A Morrison shelter pressed into service as a table. This 'refuge room' looks much like a sitting room, but the caption in 1941 praised the tea-drinkers for heeding government advice to 'prepare for winter raids'.

AIR-RAID MEMORY

'We were three days and three nights in an underground shelter in Grandad's garden. Crowded together the family were not too pleased when the local police knocked on the door and made them take in two more people who had been a mile away from their home when the air raid began, especially as they were none too clean. After the dawn broke and everyone crawled out of the shelter, not only were we covered in dust but covered in fleas from our two uninvited guests!'

Margaret Hofman, age 3 and living in London when the war started

BLACKED OUT, BOMBED OUT

Evenings at home in 1940–41 were seldom free from the drone of aircraft overhead, the thump of anti-aircraft guns, and the crashes and thuds of bombs and falling masonry. The 'all clear' sirens brought relief – but only until the next night.

At night-time, blackness descended: no street lamps; no bright shop windows; cars and buses moving cautiously with hooded headlamps. A nationwide blackout meant all windows, skylights and glazed doors had to be screened so no light showed to guide enemy planes. Shops ran out of cloth for blackout curtains, in blue and dark green as well as black. Blinds and small windows could be painted with a wash made from size, lamp-black powder and hot water. When someone forgot to switch off the hall light before opening the front door, the ARP warden's cry of 'Put that light out' passed into legend. The Home Office suggested that 'some people perhaps will only use one or two rooms at night ...' forgetting, or unaware, that few ordinary families had houses so spacious that

they could choose in which room they would pass the evening. One grand home that was bombed was Buckingham Palace; on 13 September 1940, Queen Elizabeth was removing an eyelash from King George VI's eye when a bomb exploded in the quadrangle outside.

Air raids were nerve-racking; some children found them exciting but grumbled when roused from their beds night after night. London's Swan & Edgar sold siren suits 'to keep the children warm and cosy in an emergency' for just 15s 11d (80p). By October 1940 a quarter of a million Londoners were already homeless, or 'bombed out'. When the Luftwaffe bombed Coventry on the night of 14/15 November 1940, 550 people were killed and more than 40,000 homes damaged or destroyed. Next day, vans of the Queen's Messenger Convoys, operated by the Women's Voluntary Services (WVS), brought in food and mobile canteens to feed the homeless and rescuers. Repair gangs went to work and by January 1941 around 28,000 of the damaged homes were habitable again. It was the same story in cities across the land. In May 1941 the 41 Rest Centres in Hull received nearly 10,000 homeless people in one night; all had been found temporary homes or billets within 24 hours.

After rescuers had brought out the dead and injured, and while repair squads set to work, families

◄ Blackout time in 1943. Doreen Buckner (age 7) draws the curtains at home. Her younger brother and sister had known nothing but war, and Doreen could remember 'little of pre-war life', according to a Ministry of Information feature on Britain's 'war babies'.

➤ Ready with his gun: a Home Guard volunteer gets ready for patrol, while his wife mans the kitchen in the dark days of December 1940.

A painting of a mobile canteen with firefighters and local residents. It was published in a 1944 book about the sterling work of the National Fire Service during the Blitz.

▲ Rest Centres provided hot food and shelter for those driven from their homes. King George VI and Queen Elizabeth visited children in this London Rest Centre in November 1940.

picked through the debris to see what they could salvage. Builder Bill Regan and his wife Vi, their home in London's East End badly damaged, slept in the front room 'with the table pushed up against the fireplace, and the mattress and blankets under the table'. Even a 'near-miss' shattered a home: the blast broke windows, felled walls, stripped roofs, blew out or splintered doors. High-explosive bombs and parachute landmines cut gas, electricity and water supplies; fires started by small incendiary bombs destroyed homes, as well as targeting factories and warehouses.

CRIME IN THE BLITZ

There were reports of looting after air raids: gas meters rifled, shops scavenged, thieves in Fire Party steel hats and armbands picking through bombed houses. Some people helped themselves to coal from cellars of bombed properties. The penalty for looting was technically death, but was never imposed. In 1940, 12 convicted murderers were hanged. The murder rate (115 murders in 1940, 159 in 1942, 95 in 1944) remained fairly steady.

SETTING UP HOME

Before 1939, many young couples hoped to buy or rent a house or flat of their own, perhaps on one of the new estates. The war wrecked such plans for most. Wartime weddings were short on frills but high on hope as couples set up home as best they could. Deciding where to live often meant hard choices, especially if one or both partners was conscripted for the Armed Forces or war work. Going back home to parents was a common decision – ironic, since for many single people the war meant leaving home for the first time.

Wartime weddings were often fitted into a weekend's leave. A champagne toast was a rare treat; the wedding cake might have a cardboard top to disguise the lack of sugar icing; and 'cream' for the trifle was an unfamiliar blend of margarine, powdered milk and water. Many brides got married in a two-piece suit which they could recycle for other occasions, and ' bottom drawers' were sadly lacking in both table linen and honeymoon underwear, unless a relative in the Merchant Navy

WEDDING-DAY DASHES

Wartime weddings had many unplanned moments and were often interrupted by air raids. A 1941 bride remembered 'having to keep dashing into the church crypt during the ceremony, and into the coal cellar during the reception'.

could bring back some silk or chiffon bought in New York. For wedding presents, 'something old' was far more likely than 'something new', or even 'blue'. Honeymoon options were limited. Two or three days at a seaside hotel, with barbed wire on the beaches and very little on the dinner menu, were as much as most newly-weds could hope for.

People swapped household items and trudged in and out of shops looking for the unobtainable. High street stores, like homes, bore the scars of battle: John Lewis in London's Oxford Street

▲ Anything still sellable? Staff at John Lewis in Oxford Street start to clear up after the store was bombed in 1940.

◄ Hope sprang eternal for wartime weddings. Mr and Mrs Benfield were married in August 1943; the bride wore a smart suit while her new husband made do with his battledress.

▲ Home-making often involved scouring markets, second-hand shops and war-damage sales.

ORANGE-BOX FURNITURE

'The motto was "make do and mend" and in my early childhood my bedside cabinet was an "orange box" from the greengrocer. It was made of coarsely cut unvarnished white-wood slats which gave one splinters, hammered together with a few nails ... I doubt if it had ever contained oranges, so the name was not at all appropriate.'

Pat Cryer, who was a child in Edgware, north London, during the war

was burned out in an air raid on 18 September 1940, but was partly back in business three weeks later. The bomb-site was still there in the 1950s, until a new store opened in 1960. Furniture was rationed, with furniture factories switching to war production – making aircraft, for instance.

In 1943, Utility furniture went on sale. Made from hardboard, plywood and veneers, Utility furniture looked plain (for example, chair legs were straight, not decoratively turned), but it lasted well. Priority was given to newly-weds, people with children, and those who had been bombed out.

Many couples were separated soon after they were married, sometimes for years, in some cases for ever. Urgent news, good and bad, came in a telegram. Comparatively few wartime homes had a telephone. Whatever the news, the war allowed little respite for private celebrations or for family grief.

➤ A Utility dining room, presented as part of a publicity campaign as the wartime designs went on sale to priority groups.

WARTIME KITCHENS

The typical 1930s British kitchen fell short of the gleaming kitchens in Hollywood films. Few families owned a refrigerator or washing machine, and production of such luxuries stopped during the war. With no refrigerator or freezer, housewives kept meat in a meat safe, away from flies. In hot weather, butter went runny and milk went sour, even when stored under a milk cooler or in a bucket of cold water. Fortunately the milkman delivered every day, even when he (or she) had to step over rubble to reach the doorstep.

Most small kitchens had a kitchen cabinet, a tall unit with storage space and a pull-down worktop; older kitchens often had a wooden dresser. There were wooden shelves and cupboards, and a stoneware sink with a wooden draining board. Hot water came from a kitchen range, or from a back boiler heated by a coal fire. Many homes relied on a 'geyser', a gas water-heater with a pilot light that often went out, and which roared and clanked cheerfully when it did fire into life.

The wartime home had far fewer power-points than today, especially in the kitchen. Ceiling lights dangled from fabric-covered flexes, and the same sockets were often used to plug in electric irons. Most people (over 70 per cent of home-owners in 1939) cooked on a free-standing gas stove, enamelled for easy cleaning, with three or four gas burners, a grill and oven. The latest models had a 'Regulo' number-control to set the oven temperature. Coal gas was poisonous, so leaving an unlit gas tap on was doubly dangerous, risking death by asphyxiation or explosion. Electric cookers were mostly found in flats, and electrical gadgets, other than irons, were few: a vacuum cleaner, toaster or electric kettle was a luxury. 'Putting the kettle on' meant boiling water on the gas stove.

Automatic washing machines were not sold in Britain until the 1950s, so unless it was sent to the laundry the weekly wash was done by hand. But the drudgery of wartime washdays was eased a little by a gas boiler to heat the water, and perhaps

▼ The centrepiece of the 1940s kitchen was the cooker, usually a gas stove. This kitchen is in a prefab, now preserved at the Avoncroft Museum near Bromsgrove, Worcestershire.

▼ All clear for the next meal. In September 1940 a housewife peels the vegetables for dinner, with plenty of fresh air through shattered windows. Such photos were published to encourage the 'carry on' spirit.

GUINNESS for STRENGTH

▲ Guinness was good for you in many respects; this advertisement supported the Dig For Victory campaign.

> Cooks experimented with the novel and uncertain delights of powdered dried eggs, a dozen per packet.

the aid of a dolly or washboard. Soaking wet sheets and towels were put through a mangle, before being pegged on the line outdoors, or hung up in the kitchen. To 'air', clothes were placed on a wooden clothes horse in front of the fire.

In 1940 households were asked not to hoard food, since even if the Nazis invaded 'the government has made arrangements for food supplies'. Most people kept a small stock (which might include tins of soup, peas and meat, powdered milk, and packets of tea and flour) for an emergency. When houswives went shopping, as most did every day in the village, high street or corner shop, they bought whatever they could get and afford. Queuing outside shops became part of the weary business of putting a meal on the table. Familiar household products were sold in wartime austerity packaging, but promised extra benefits: Puritan soap gave 'double-ration lather', while Fry's chocolate spread 'solves the butter problem'. Mazawattee tea came in a 'gas-proof' tin, and in Smith's crisps, despite the sombre wartime packet, it was reassuring to know that the 'contents remain unchanged'. But food and drink promised a pick-me-up: a cup of hot Bovril made you feel 'warm-and-cheery rather than cold-and-weary'. A glass of Guinness was, according to 'a doctor', 'a wonderful help to women', bringing 'new strength to tired limbs'. To keep going, and still look your best, all you needed was the right tonic, if the advertisements were to be believed.

MEAGRE RATIONS

It was announced in November 1939 that food rationing would commence on 8 January 1940. Bacon, butter and sugar were the first items to be restricted, and others were added as the months progressed. Amounts varied depending on availability but when rationing was at its height a typical weekly allowance for an adult was:

1 egg (and 1 pack dried egg monthly)
2oz (55g) cheese
2oz (55g) tea
2oz (55g) butter
4oz (115g) cooking fat/margarine
4oz (115g) bacon/ham
8oz (225g) sugar
12oz (350g) sweets (monthly)
1lb (450g) jam (every one or two months)
3 pints (1.5 litres) milk
1s 2d (6p) meat (rationed by price not weight)

▲ A wartime food ration book. Designated shops were shown on the left-hand page.

For women in particular, 'what to wear' mattered almost as much as 'what to eat.' Clothes rationing was introduced in June 1941. At first, to buy herself a coat a woman had to hand over 15 coupons; by 1943 the year's clothing ration per person was only 40 coupons. Bedrooms that escaped bomb damage held few fashion surprises. Chests of drawers and wardrobes remained barren of exciting new purchases, in rooms where curtains and rugs were usually the same ones that had been there in 1939, and where redecoration remained a distant fantasy. Advertising copy was upbeat: Yardley telling customers in 1942 that 'our faces must never reflect personal troubles'; Berlei warning that 'it's bad for morale to let figures go'.

▲ A 1944 advertisement promoting Utility clothing, and careful shopping.

▼ Norman Hartnell Utility designs for the summer of 1943.

Winter warmth was as hard to come by as frilly underwear and the nimble-fingered turned blankets into coats, and parachute silk (if they could get it) into knickers. Home dressmaking had been popular since the 1920s and sewing machines clicked busily. So did knitting needles. 'Let your national service be knitting' trumpeted a Sirdar wool advertisement, and woollen hats, balaclavas, scarves, mittens, socks, cardigans, pullovers, blanket squares, vests and baby clothes poured forth. Clothes sent from the United States as 'Bundles for Britain' were welcomed, but some women preferred to unpick donated knitwear, wash the wool and knit it again to patterns of their own choice. Worn sheets and blankets were cut down the middle and sewn 'sides to middle' for a new lease of life. Eiderdowns kept people snug on chilly nights; only those few Britons who had spent winter holidays abroad had slept beneath a duvet.

➤ 'Ideal wear for children' from a 1939 catalogue, when 'breechette sets' were popular.

> The Civilian Clothing Act of 1941 (CC41) logo, known as 'the two cheeses'.

In 1942 the Board of Trade announced the Utility clothing scheme, and the Utility 'two cheeses' logo was soon familiar on a range of items from coats and shoes to blankets. Leading lights of the fashion world such as Hardy Amies and Norman Hartnell contributed Utility designs, intended to combine quality, economy and functionality. There was no waste or frippery: jackets with no more than three buttons, shoe heels no more than 2 inches (5cm) high, skirts with no more than four knife-edged pleats.

The 'Make Do and Mend' campaign of 1943 encouraged everyone to restyle old clothes, for example by making a skirt from a pair of trousers, or adding sleeves to a waistcoat to turn it into a jacket. Socks were darned; elbows of jackets were patched; and worn hankies stitched (the tissue had yet to reach Britain). Before the war a box of

▲ Make Do and Mend posters urged people to give old clothes a new lease of life, to 'save buying new'.

hankies cost 1s 11d (10p); by 1944, it was close to 7 shillings (35p). Nylon stockings were almost impossible to find, as was elastic – therefore many women wore French knickers with buttons. Boiler suits with bib tops, as worn for factory work, were off-ration but hardly glamorous. A woman felt better if she could afford a Jaeger herringbone Utility suit, costing between £4 and £5.

TROUSERS IN VOGUE

In wartime, trousers (or 'slacks') became essential wear for many working women, costing around £4 (and 8 ration coupons). Some magazines thought trousers suitable only for gardening. In 1943 *The Lady* described slacks as 'sloppy and unsuitable' for town wear, and equally wrong for 'fat women' and 'women pushing prams'.

◄ Fashion magazines highlighted the trend for practical women's clothing. This driving suit, featured in *Harper's Bazaar* in 1939, was tailored at the back to allow 'for cranking and other violent exercise'.

TURN ON THE NEWS

▲ The radio news was often grim – though to listen to the wireless while holding gas masks, as in this photograph from 1939, would have struck many families later in the war as absurd.

War news dominated the airwaves and the newspapers. The radio (or wireless) held pride of place in many homes, usually in the warmest room. Many families kept their front room for Sundays and visitors, eating and relaxing in the back room, the only room with a fire. The fire was seldom blazing, for 'heaping on the coal' was tantamount to being a Nazi agent. Bedrooms and bathrooms were glacial: bedside glasses of water froze overnight, and baths were hurried affairs – especially when you had only 5 inches (12.5cm) of bathwater to sit in.

BBC television broadcasts had started in 1936 but stopped when war broke out. The BBC radio news bulletins became part of the daily routine, and included battlefront reports from its war correspondents such as Richard Dimbleby and Wynford Vaughan-Thomas. Families also gathered to listen to the broadcasts by Winston Churchill, the king's Christmas message, and each evening the BBC's output of talks, comedy shows and music for most tastes. Listening to the wireless was a shared family occasion hard to imagine today, and the radio itself in its polished cabinet was an object of pride, with knobs to twiddle, glowing dials and valves, and exotic-sounding foreign stations. Many people tuned in to *Germany Calling* and the propaganda of 'Lord Haw-Haw' (William Joyce), though in some homes this was regarded as almost treasonable.

Almost matching the wireless as a status symbol, though only in better-off homes, was the radiogram, a cabinet containing a radio and electric gramophone. Most homes made do with a cheaper

◄ Ministry of Information publications found their way into many homes. This HMSO book from 1941 described the RAF's bombing offensive.

▲ Women's magazines gave a stream of ideas for home-making, and also showed women in new and often adventurous wartime roles.

GOVERNMENT ADVICE

If you caught a cold it was your duty to 'trap the germs in your handkerchief'. Posters urged people to walk rather than use public transport, and to wage war on the wasteful 'Squander Bug'. If a train was delayed, don't ask why: 'the censor says you must not know, when there's been a fall of snow'. 'Walls had ears', and the impression given was that enemy spies lurked everywhere, though in fact almost all German agents in Britain were swiftly arrested.

▲ The Squander Bug, a cartoon Nazi nasty, warned people not to waste money or precious resources.

and smaller wind-up gramophone to play their 78 rpm records. Winding up the gramophone while a record was still spinning made Gracie Fields, Richard Tauber or Bing Crosby gabble at speed, much to the amusement of children.

War news was discussed over the dinner table and around the fireside; war maps in newspapers were pored over; anti-Hitler cartoons chuckled at; household hints snipped out and saved. There were even reports of wartime soccer matches, with star players now in the Forces turning out for teams wherever they were posted. Despite paper shortages, there was plenty to read: national and local newspapers, photo-news magazines such as *Picture Post* and *John Bull*, women's magazines including *Woman's Weekly* and *Woman and Home*, children's comics, and paperback books (a 1930s innovation). And every year hundreds of government leaflets dropped onto doormats – advising householders how to save this and recycle that, keep healthy and keep secrets, turn carrots into cakes, potatoes into pies, and generally do their bit to help win the war.

The BBC played a part on the garden front, encouraging people to 'Dig for Victory' with its own wartime garden and gardening expert, Mr Middleton, who gave tips *In Your Garden* every Sunday afternoon on the wireless. In many homes an Anderson shelter squatted where the peacetime lawn had been; enterprising gardeners turned the shelter roof into a vegetable plot. People without gardens were urged to cultivate allotments, and there were vegetable plots in parks and other open spaces, even in the dry moat at the Tower of London.

Before the war Britain had imported much food from abroad but the shipping lifeline was threatened by German submarines preying on merchant ship convoys. With shipping space desperately needed for fuel, vehicles and guns, the nation had to produce more home-grown food.

The Ministry of Food wanted Britons to switch from growing flowers to vegetables, and the 'grow your own' campaign introduced 'Doctor Carrot' and 'Potato Pete'. People who had never dug a potato or planted a pansy in a pot became horticulturalists, swapping tips on how to make a compost heap, grow peas and beans, combat greenfly and make fruit preserves. The keep-fit element was symbolized by a Dig for Victory song which began: 'Dig! Dig! Dig! And your muscles will grow big.'

Gardening – once a private hobby, or a sought-after job in a large house or municipal park – became a public demonstration of commitment to the national war effort. So did hunting beaches and fields for wild food – anything from unlikely seaweed to more appetizing blackberries. WVS volunteers on 'herb drives' collected nettles for animal feed, foxgloves to make the drug digitalis, and hips to make rose-hip syrup. Many suburban gardens sprouted not just vegetables but also rabbit hutches and chicken runs (rabbits were raised for meat, chickens for eggs and meat). Food scraps went into pig bins at the end of the road.

⌃   This 1943 poster urged people to Dig for Victory. The campaign sent millions of new gardeners out with spades, trowels and packets of seeds.

⌃   Doctor Carrot, nattily dressed in spats and top hat, led the campaign to eat more carrots, and so keep the wartime household in tip-top shape.

Pigs ate anything, townsfolk with scant knowledge of farming were informed, except coffee grounds, rhubarb leaves and fishbones.

With a record six million acres of farmland being cultivated, food production increased, and there were gluts of potatoes and carrots. The Ministry of Food urged families to eat more of these available foods, rather than dream of pineapples and bananas. New recipes showed how to cook the more mundane vegetables in new and ingenious ways, though Carrotade (a drink made from carrot and swede juice) never really caught on, even when the government suggested that eating carrots helped you see better at night in the blackout.

▲ Dandelion leaves from the 'wild larder' made a tasty salad, as shown in this 1941 *Picture Post* photograph.

DIY OPTIONS

While gardening provided much-needed relaxation for some, and a chance to forget wartime worries by retreating to the garden shed or allotment, others did a bit of DIY around the house. However, the range of DIY products was severely limited, and boiling glue in a can or mixing home-made distemper was not to everyone's liking.

▼ Cabbage-growing could be portrayed as patriotic, fun and even glamorous – as in this 1944 photo.

COUNTRY LIFE

▲ Small London evacuees climb the steps to their new wartime home, a country house in Cheltenham, Gloucestershire.

In 1939 the powers-that-be feared that air raids might cause mass panic, and the Whitehall view was that city children should be evacuated to the countryside. In the first few weeks of war 1.5 million people were moved by bus or train. The evacuation experience could be an eye-opener for host and homesick children alike. Some city children had never seen 'real live cows' and were shocked to see where milk came from, and equally surprised to learn that carrots and peas did not grow in tins.

Rural Britain largely escaped the worst of the Blitz, and country cottages and farmhouses were reasonably well-equipped to cope with wartime privations; many country people were used to oil lamps, candles, kitchen ranges, log fires and water from a well, and the privy (lavatory) at the

bottom of the garden was unlikely to be destroyed by enemy action. With kitchen gardens, pigs and chickens, a rod or net for fishing, and a gun to provide rabbit, pigeon, pheasant or partridge, the country kitchen usually offered more varied fare. May Chalmers, wife of the Sheriff of Oban in Scotland, did not feel the pinch until 1942; she told journalist Mea Allan that, having just learned to

➤ Teddy Neale, a London evacuee, brings home rabbits for supper in the Cotswolds. Teddy, his sister and mother were billeted on a local farm.

cook, she found the Sunday roast could be made to last a week. Putting the house on a war footing for the Chalmers meant sacking the garden boy and two maids, and shutting up the dining room to take their meals in the pantry.

Owners of some large country homes gave parties to evacuee children and tea to American airmen. Other large country houses were taken over by schools; some became hospitals, administrative centres, or billets for the Forces. Bletchley Park in Buckinghamshire, in 1938 a Victorian mansion about to be demolished for housing development, became Station X, secret headquarters of MI6's code-breakers who when they first moved in pretended to be 'Captain Ridley's shooting party'.

Petrol shortages put a brake on non-essential driving. By 1942, with private cars banned, most drivers had laid up their vehicles 'for the duration' of the war. Farmers ploughed with horses, and a few dog-carts and pony-traps creaked back into service. Many plans had to be put on hold. In 1939 Winston Churchill had been planning a butterfly house at his Kent country home, Chartwell. It was 1946 before the wartime Prime Minister saw his butterflies become reality. Much had happened in the meantime.

▲ Life in town and country was very hard for many. This Welsh woman in 1944 scrubbed the washing in a tin bath in her backyard.

LOST VILLAGE

The village of Tyneham in Dorset was taken over by the Army in 1943 for training purposes. Its 252 residents had to pack up and leave, and their houses were stripped. Tyneham became a ghost village, though its church and school were later refurbished as a museum. The village remains Ministry of Defence property on the Lulworth military ranges.

▼ Bletchley Park in the 1930s. During the Second World War, the house became a top-secret intelligence-gathering site.

▼ Winston Churchill at home at Chartwell in 1939, standing to work at his high-level desk.

◄ A wartime house with a sign inviting passers-by to come in 'if you are caught out in a raid'. The owner's shelter had room for two guests.

Front doors opened frequently in wartime, to family, friends, neighbours and passing strangers, and the hat-stand in the hall was hung with many hats and coats, including uniform greatcoats, caps and berets. Britain in the 1940s was a nation of hat-wearers, winter and summer, and in winter a nation of coat-wearers since most people were outdoors in all weathers: queuing outside shops, fire-watching on windy roofs, waiting for buses and trains, walking to and from work. Wartime suitcases and military kitbags made many journeys, and wartime shoes tramped many miles.

Neighbours popped in to drink tea, exchange news and share the pleasure of an airmail letter or postcard from a son or daughter overseas. When troubles came, there was usually someone on hand to help and with whom to share the sorrow. Air raids brought good neighbourliness to the fore

and, while it is possible to exaggerate the wartime spirit of 'togetherness', many people did their best to help in a common emergency. They took hot meals to homes without gas, lent blankets and sweaters for chilly nights, offered a bed or an armchair to people made homeless or stranded by transport breakdowns, and helped clear up the morning after a raid.

The familiar view from many windows changed overnight, as bombs reshaped the landscape: a neighbour's home reduced to a heap of bricks, dust and charred timbers; a friend's furniture piled in the street; a bomb crater in the back garden. Such sights left people with mixed feelings: sadness for the loss, relief to have survived. Many survivors buried their worst memories, preferring to talk only of the absurd and the amusing wartime incidents – of which there were many.

Never before had so many Britons moved home so much. There were more than 60 million changes of address during the war. As people watched their homes becoming shabbier, battered by bombing and starved of improvement by rationing and shortages, they wondered about the future. Many families had simply been thankful for a roof over their heads, even if the wallpaper and paint were the same as when they moved in 10 or 15 years before. By 1944 the end of the war seemed in sight, and people began to think and read about the future: 'Homes for Tomorrow' were pictured as wide avenues of new houses in bright sunlight across green fields. In this Utopia a new carpet seemed a modest wish, for families were promised that, very soon, when peacetime production resumed, shops would have all manner of appliances for the home – and that to make sure of their washing machine and refrigerator, would-be purchasers should add their names to priority order lists without delay. The view was about to change again.

MUSEUM ON THE MOVE

To escape the bombs, the Natural History Museum in London sent its geology specimens to Tattershall Castle in Lincolnshire. Fawley Court near Henley in Oxfordshire received cases of the museum's insects and plants, even though the owners stayed on in the house. The grounds of the Natural History Museum were dug up for vegetables, and the Special Operations Executive took over deserted galleries to test exploding rats and other curious secret-service devices.

⋏ People made new friends through civil defence service and war work. Here members of the London Auxiliary Ambulance Service relax off-duty in 1940.

⋎ This man took his dog for a walk and returned to find his home in ruins and his wife dead, after a V1 hit in 1944. A policeman tried to offer some comfort.

⋎ Civil defence and rescue teams search through the rubble of a destroyed building in 1944.

Christmas 1940 was grim. In December that year the food ration for 'harder-living Britain' had been cut still further. Lord Woolton, Minister of Food, announced that imports of tinned fruit and all fresh fruit except oranges would cease, since he was informed 'on the best scientific authority that the nation can do without them'. That winter of 1940–41 was the coldest that most people could remember.

Getting home for a wartime Christmas, for those who had leave and could travel, meant long waits at stations and many hours on slow, crowded trains. Homecomings were joyful, even if the decorations did look a trifle faded and war-torn.

◄ Home for Christmas. A soldier gets a warm welcome as he comes home on leave. The war meant separation, often for years, for many couples.

CHRISTMAS CAKE CHEER

With dried fruit in short supply, one tip was to add gravy browning to the Christmas cake mixture to give it a rich colour, in an effort to disguise the lack of juicy sultanas, raisins and currants. A mock-marzipan covering could be made using haricot beans, soaked then dried in the oven and pushed through a sieve to replace the essential ground almonds.

◄ Selfridge's window in Oxford Street, London, was sandbagged for Christmas 1939, but Father Christmas had turned up as usual.

▲ Christmas in an Anderson shelter, 1940. Fortunately Father Christmas and his sleigh seem to have avoided the anti-aircraft guns.

Toasts were drunk, with whatever refreshment was available, to 'absent friends'. Christmas cakes without icing were given paper frills instead, and if they could not get a Christmas tree people decorated twigs dipped in paint. Fading pre-war paper streamers and other decorations were carefully unpacked from pre-war boxes, but many glass baubles did not survive being shaken up by air raids, so some families had to hang their trees with coloured buttons, earrings and twists of silver paper. Party hats could be home-made, but party make-up was often in short supply. One tip was to melt down the stubs of lipsticks, mix the paste with cold cream and use it as rouge.

Christmas cards were smaller and less fancy than those on sale before the war, but just as welcome. There were no Christmas lights in the high street, and shop displays were underwhelming. It was hard to feel Christmassy in the blackout – a far cry from today, when so many houses are ablaze with outside lights through December. Christmas gifts might have to be wrapped in newspaper, but people managed to find stocking-treats for children, even chocolate – and an orange in the toe of the stocking was always welcome. With toyshops short of stock, many people made toy wooden planes and stuffed knitted animals to give as gifts, or repainted a discarded doll's pram or pedal tricycle to delight a new young owner.

▲ A Christmas party for the community. Wartime relaxed some social barriers, though not all.

WVS toy exchanges were useful too: here families could swap toys and books. Annuals were welcome even in wartime guises: Alfred Bestall's ever-popular *Rupert*, *Radio Fun* with Arthur Askey and other BBC stars, or *Film Fun* with Laurel and Hardy and star-casts of Hollywood favourites.

Magazines, as ever, were full of advice: how to make the sitting room feel cosy 'in spite of that empty chair'; how to get the most from the wartime Christmas kitchen by preparing a 'Santa Claus salad' made with cabbage; and 'Goose with One Leg', a stuffed leg of mutton. Few opted to put Woolton pie on the Christmas table: carrots, onions and other vegetables topped with mashed potatoes made a nutritious, but hardly festive, dish.

CHILDREN'S WAR

Children in Dover, Kent, play in the street, March 1941. The coastal town was a frequent target for enemy air attacks.

A child about to start school in September 1939 was entering secondary school by the time the war ended. The school leaving age was 14, so many teenagers went to work, often waiting – unless they were in a reserved occupation – to be 'called up' (conscripted) for the forces between the ages of 18 and 20. Schools stayed open, though some moved their pupils and staff to new premises in the countryside, and national exams continued – to many children's dismay.

With parents often exhausted, overworked or away, many children roamed streets and fields, and had far more freedom than most children today. Older children were left to care for younger siblings and mothers happily sent youngsters to the corner shop for groceries. Scouts cycled around looking for bomb-craters, and children of all ages collected shrapnel (from anti-aircraft gun shells) and anything that looked like bits of shot-down enemy planes. They played on bomb sites, which was extremely dangerous: many ruined sites were unsafe, and unexploded bombs remained a buried menace for years after the war. In the largely bomb-free countryside, evacuees generally made friends with the locals, after the occasional ritual fight, and became used to country ways: 'we have candles here', one evacuee wrote home, in a tone of resignation.

In the cities most children coped well, sleeping through air raids and in the shelters, though often keeping weary adults awake with cheerful prattle about 'that was a close one' as a bomb exploded. Children's health was better than pre-war, thanks to having little sugar, less fat, more vegetables and, from 1942, free cod liver oil and orange juice.

> Chocolate was a wartime treat, often repackaged but still recognizable and doubly welcome.

▲ Children's comics often portrayed plucky youngsters defying the enemy, in this instance the Japanese.

AN EVACUEE REMEMBERS

'[The] cottage that we occupied … had a water tap outside the front door in the street, and it was my job to keep the cottage water supply going by regularly filling a small milk churn. It was also my task to keep a supply of water for the outside toilet, which was down the very bottom of a very large garden. In the terraced cottage next door lived Mr and Mrs Kingdom who regularly supplied us with fresh vegetables and now and again a brace of rabbits with the odd chicken from time to time.'

Wally Sullivan, evacuated from London to Witheridge, Devon

They were fit, too: most walked to and from school. Children's clothes were a problem; many growing youngsters made do with hand-me-downs, and WVS clothing exchanges were kept busy even after the war ended.

Toys reflected children's wartime experiences. Painting books had pictures of soldiers, sailors and pilots, and jigsaws depicted victories such as the naval Battle of the River Plate. Children studied aircraft-recognition books, and most could tell a Dornier from a Junkers overhead. They played war card games, board games and dart games ('see if you can hit Adolf'), and dressed dolls in the uniforms of every service. They fought battles with die-cast metal bombers and matchstick-firing tanks, flew wooden scale-model Spitfires, and built pontoon bridges and bulldozers from Meccano.

When not playing, doing homework, or listening to *ITMA* (It's That Man Again) on the wireless, children buried their heads in a favourite comic. There was a host to choose from, including *The Hotspur, Boy's Own Paper, The Champion, The Rover, The Wizard, Girls' Crystal, Sunny Stories, Tiny Tots, The Rainbow* and *The Beano*. Popular children's writers put their heroes into wartime settings: Richmal Crompton's William carrying on his escapades in *William and the Evacuees* and *William Does His Bit*, and W. E. Johns' daring pilot doing his bit in *Biggles Defies the Swastika* and other thrillers.

▼ Help around the house: a little boy sweeps up while his mother dries socks above the stove.

STILL MORE

BONES

WANTED FOR

SALVAGE

When rubber supplies from the Far East dried up after Japan entered the war in 1941, rubber toys, balls, hot-water bottles, old tyres, bath mats, even bathing caps were sacrificed. In 1943 more than 50 million unwanted books were collected for pulping. Who knows how many rare first editions were to disappear?

The household fire was a reassuring comfort but constantly under threat from coal shortages. Many families tried to economize; they swept up the coal dust from the floor of the coal bunker into empty sugar cartons, to make 'brickettes' for burning. They tried burning a blend of tea leaves and coal dust, and placed bricks or lumps of chalk at the back of the fire to conserve and radiate extra heat. Although people became used to the lights going out and the gas going off, they were also reassured that repairs were usually done swiftly, and life went on.

◀ This 1940 poster from the Ministry of Information encouraged people to save bones, used to make explosives.

▼ WVS members collect aluminium pots and pans for salvage in 1940.

The wartime household was always short of something. People ran out of soap, ink, paper, setting lotion, hairpins, even toilet rolls. Those who stocked up with toilet rolls in 1939 ran out in a year or so. There was a brief outbreak of 'toilet roll panic' in 1944, when some shops limited customers to two rolls each.

To keep the wartime home in the vanguard of the war effort, and reduce waste, the government launched national campaigns to 'salvage'. Salvage carts collected paper, bones, scrap metal, old records, glass jars, rubber and rags for recycling. Children went around with handcarts asking for unwanted saucepans which, they assured the donors, would end up in a Spitfire. Metal railings and park gates were melted down.

Buses and trains kept running, and people turned up for work as usual. People washed the bomb-dust from their curtains, cleaned their windows (if they had any left), swept and scrubbed the front step, watered the seedling cabbages, went shopping and made dinner. They had babies too. What else could they do, except carry on, in the hope that one day it would be over?

D-Day (6 June 1944) lifted everyone's spirits. The Allied invasion of France seemed to herald victory, and the lifting of blackout regulations in September 1944 was another sign that, at last, the end might be in sight. The arrival of V1 and V2 missiles over London that summer was a reminder that the war was not yet over, and hundreds of homes fell victim to a renewed – but final – onslaught from the air. There would be even more rebuilding when peace finally came.

KEEPING UP APPEARANCES

London's top hotels such as the Savoy still served six-course dinners, despite rationing – and even though steel girders supported the ceilings and sandbags lined walls and corridors, Carroll Gibbons and his band played hits of the day such as 'A Nightingale Sang in Berkeley Square'. The hotel provided mattresses and pillows in the basement for dinner guests forced to shelter during a raid.

∧ A woman in Northampton uses water saved in a metal bath; water restrictions often made home life and chores very testing.

∧ Communal feeding centres at schools, like this one in central London, offered affordable meals to families unable to cook at home.

Civil servants and architects looked ahead to a brave new post-war landscape. The writer George Orwell was less sanguine; in a 1944 essay, he predicted that the post-war world would probably be 'a ghastly muddle'. In his view, 'everyone wants, above all things, a rest'.

Wartime fatigue ate into optimism. Working long shifts, waiting for trains and buses, queuing at shops: the daily round was hard on body, mind and nerves. Mass Observation (a volunteer-run social research project started in 1937) interviewed people and reported a widespread feeling that peacetime Britain would be 'the same old story', despite all the 'talk and propaganda about town planning'. Critics said planners were talking

∧ Many prefabs lasted much longer than the planned 10 years – like this one in Cleveland, north-east England, still a home 60 years after it was built.

to one another, not listening to 'the masses', and that reconstruction committees seemed more interested in 'precincts' than traditional shops. Architects painted a rosy picture of 'residential districts designed on the garden city principle': elegant flats and modern houses amid green landscapes with new roads, schools, libraries, sports fields and theatres. Here was a seductive vision to war-weary people: 'more leisure, new interests within the comfortable and healthy precincts of our new homes'. And those new homes would be 'all-electric' with electric cocktail shakers, illuminated flower table decorations, underfloor heating, air conditioning and food-warmers on the dining table.

Most expected less. People living in slum tenements dreamed of simple comforts, such as a kitchen they could eat their meals in, their own bathroom with linoleum on the floor, and cheerful wallpaper rather than peeling paint and damp walls. A garden seemed too much to hope for, but many did. Space, fresh air and privacy:

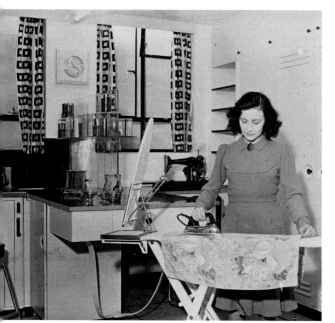

∧ As the war ended, 'modern homes' exhibitions showed families what they might hope for in the future. But years of austerity lay ahead.

> The way things were; houses in Hoxton, east London, photographed soon after the Second World War ended.

these were now sought-after, so it was hardly surprising that more than 50 per cent of people questioned chose suburban living over the inner city, and only one in 20 wanted a flat. In 1944 the government announced plans for half a million 'prefabs'; 160,000 of the factory-built homes were actually built, but many local authorities built flats instead. Flats outnumbered houses five to one in the post-war housing programme, with its new towns and 'overspill' schemes. The desire for a home (and ideally a house) of one's own was to remain a feature of British life, and politics, for the next half century and more. By 1946 the cost of a new owner-occupied home was rising – a house that had cost under £600 in 1938 was now £1,500.

Victory in the summer of 1945 was celebrated with parties, parades and religious services. Homes were hung with flags, and filled with joy at home-comings. Once the parties were over, uncertainty returned. Overheard by a journalist, a woman on a bus voiced her thoughts to her companion: it was nice to go to bed without bombs falling but 'I can't seem to feel easy, either. It's peace, I tell myself, but somehow it don't feel like peace ought to feel.' Only time would tell if the wartime spirit could survive the rebuilding and the social changes, or if it would vanish along with gas masks, ration books and the wartime house.

> Victory in Europe in May 1945 brought people out of their homes and onto the streets for parties.

Thousands of families still live in 'wartime houses' all over Britain, though few homes retain authentic 1940s features after decades of rebuilding and improvement. While redevelopment has changed the wartime landscape, and memories fade, domestic life in the Second World War is recalled and conserved in heritage sites and museums around the country. Here are contact details for a selection of places with fascinating and often stirring stories to tell about life in Britain during the war years.

Bletchley Park, The Mansion, Bletchley Park, Milton Keynes, Buckinghamshire MK3 6EB; 01908 640404; www.bletchleypark.org.uk

Clifford Road Air Raid Shelter Museum, Clifford Road, Ipswich, Suffolk IP4 1PJ; 01473 251605 (01473 431156 during school holidays); www.cliffordroadshelter.org.uk

Eden Camp Modern History Theme Museum, Malton, North Yorkshire YO17 6RT; 01653 697777; www.edencamp.co.uk

The Forties Experience, Lincolnsfields Children's Centre, Bushey Hall Drive, Bushey, Hertfordshire WD23 2ES; 01923 233841; www.fortiesexperience.co.uk

Home Front Museum, New Street, Llandudno, Clwyd LL30 2YF; 01492 871032; www.homefrontmuseum.co.uk

Imperial War Museum: Churchill War Rooms, Clive Steps, King Charles Street, London SW1A 2AQ; 020 7930 6961; http://cwr.iwm.org.uk

Imperial War Museum London, Lambeth Road, London SE1 6HZ; 020 7416 5000; www.iwm.org.uk

Imperial War Museum North, The Quays, Trafford Wharf Road, Manchester M17 1TZ; 0161 836 4000; http://north.iwm.org.uk

Milestones (Living History Museum), Churchill Way West, Basingstoke, Hampshire RG22 6PG; 01256 477766; www3.hants.gov.uk/milestones

Museum of London, 150 London Wall, London EC2Y 5HN; 020 7001 9844; www.museumoflondon.org.uk

National War Museum, Edinburgh Castle, Edinburgh EH1 2NG; 0300 123 6789; www.nms.ac.uk/our_museums/war_museum.aspx

RAF Museums:
RAF Museum London, Grahame Park Way, London NW9 5LL; 020 8205 2266; www.rafmuseum.org.uk/london

RAF Museum Cosford, Shifnal, Shropshire TF11 8UP; 01902 376 200; www.rafmuseum.org.uk/cosford

▲ Many women combined home chores with vital war work, as recreated here at the Churchill War Rooms in London.

Royal Armouries Museums:
Fort Nelson, Portsdown Hill Road, Fareham, Hampshire PO17 6AN; 01329 233 734; www.royalarmouries.org/visit-us/fort-nelson

Armouries Drive, Leeds, West Yorkshire LS10 1LT; 0113 220 1999; www.royalarmouries.org/visit-us/leeds

Tyneham Village, near Wareham, Dorset; 01929 404819; http://purbeck.nmspace.net/site/attractions/tyneham-village-p136333

Winston Churchill's Britain at War Experience, 66 Tooley Street, London SE1 2TF; 020 7403 3171; www.britainatwar.co.uk

National Trust

Chartwell, Mapleton Road, Westerham, Kent TN16 1PS; 01732 866368; www.nationaltrust.org.uk/main/w-chartwell

Croome Park, near High Green, Worcester, Worcestershire WR8 9DW; 01905 371006; www.nationaltrust.org.uk/main/w-croomepark

Information correct at time of going to press.